Mental Maths 2

Anita Straker

CAMBRIDGE
UNIVERSITY PRESS

1a

1. $60 - 5$.
2. 4×4.
3. $19 + 7$.
4. How much is 100 pence?
5. $3 + \square = 11$.
6. $10 \div 2$.
7. What is next: 15, 20, 25, 30 …?
8. 7 plus 8 minus 5.
9. Round 41 to the nearest 10.
10. $4 + 4 + 0$.

1b

1. What must you take from 17 to leave 9?
2. How much flour is on the scale pan?

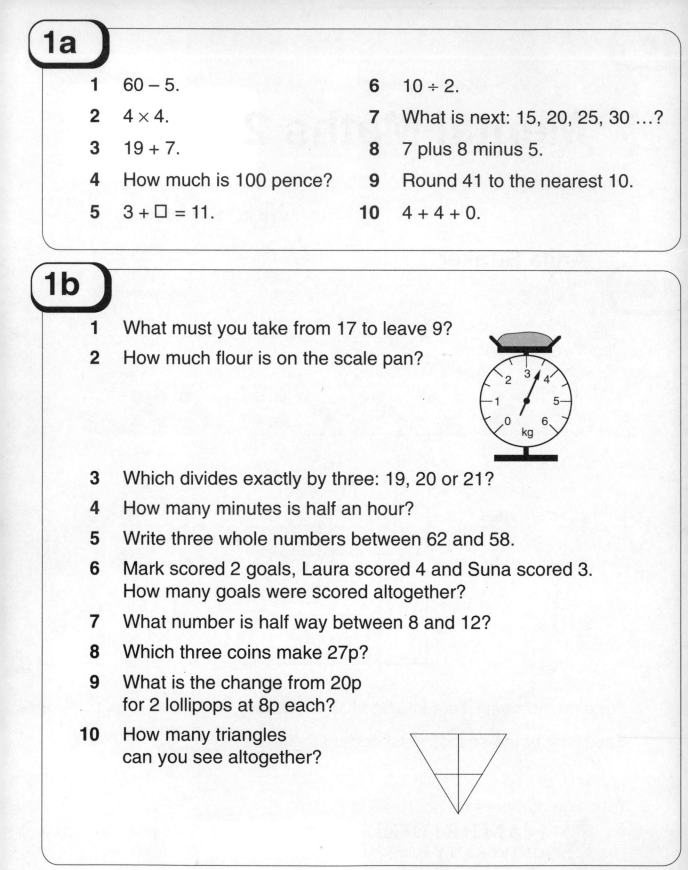

3. Which divides exactly by three: 19, 20 or 21?
4. How many minutes is half an hour?
5. Write three whole numbers between 62 and 58.
6. Mark scored 2 goals, Laura scored 4 and Suna scored 3. How many goals were scored altogether?
7. What number is half way between 8 and 12?
8. Which three coins make 27p?
9. What is the change from 20p for 2 lollipops at 8p each?
10. How many triangles can you see altogether?

1c

1. 6 + 18.
2. □ + 5 = 15.
3. 14 − 5.
4. How many days in May?
5. 5 × 5.
6. What shape is a 6-sided dice?
7. 2 + 9 − 11.
8. Which two coins make 60p?
9. 3 + 14 + 3.
10. Round 98 to the nearest 10.

1d

Use these dominoes.

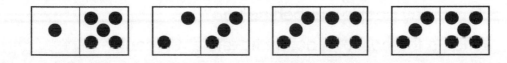

Copy this square.

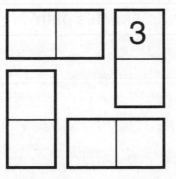

Write the number of domino spots in the boxes.

Each side of the square must add up to 10.

Touching numbers do not need to match.

2a

1 How many right angled corners has this shape?

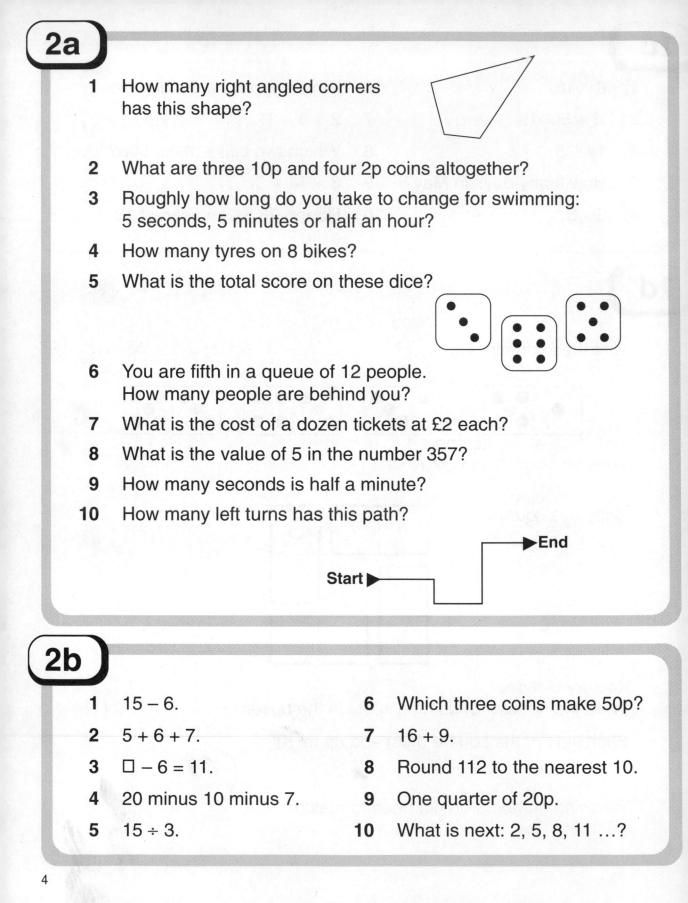

2 What are three 10p and four 2p coins altogether?

3 Roughly how long do you take to change for swimming: 5 seconds, 5 minutes or half an hour?

4 How many tyres on 8 bikes?

5 What is the total score on these dice?

6 You are fifth in a queue of 12 people. How many people are behind you?

7 What is the cost of a dozen tickets at £2 each?

8 What is the value of 5 in the number 357?

9 How many seconds is half a minute?

10 How many left turns has this path?

Start ▶   ▶End

2b

1 $15 - 6$.

2 $5 + 6 + 7$.

3 $\square - 6 = 11$.

4 20 minus 10 minus 7.

5 $15 \div 3$.

6 Which three coins make 50p?

7 $16 + 9$.

8 Round 112 to the nearest 10.

9 One quarter of 20p.

10 What is next: 2, 5, 8, 11 …?

2c

1. 7 + 17.
2. One more than 189.
3. 8 + □ = 13.
4. 9 plus 8 minus 6.
5. 16 − 7.
6. Write 353 to the nearest 10.
7. 2 × □ = 8.
8. Which four coins make 33p?
9. How many days in a year?
10. Three quarters of 40.

2d

Copy the diagram.

Use each of the numbers 1 to 6.
Write one number in every circle.

Numbers joined by lines must
differ by at least 2.

Now try this one.

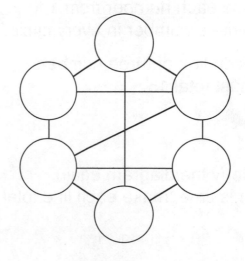

1 2 3 4 5 6

3a

1. Find the difference between a dozen and a score.
2. Put in order, least first: 86, 68, 88, 66.
3. Does David weigh 400 g or 40 kg?
4. Write **four hundred and nine** in figures.
5. What length is shown on this ruler?

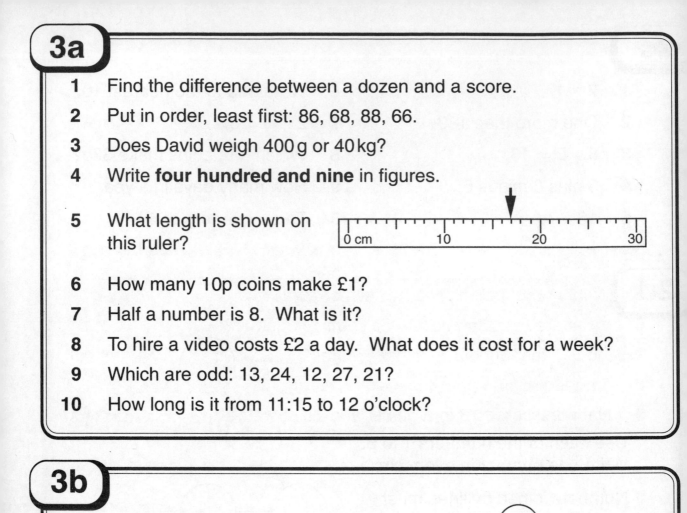

6. How many 10p coins make £1?
7. Half a number is 8. What is it?
8. To hire a video costs £2 a day. What does it cost for a week?
9. Which are odd: 13, 24, 12, 27, 21?
10. How long is it from 11:15 to 12 o'clock?

3b

Copy the diagram.

Use each number from 1 to 9.
Write a number in every circle.

Each line of three numbers
must total 15.

Copy the diagram again.
This time, make each line total 12.

1 2 3 4 5 6 7 8 9

3c

1   What is this shape called?

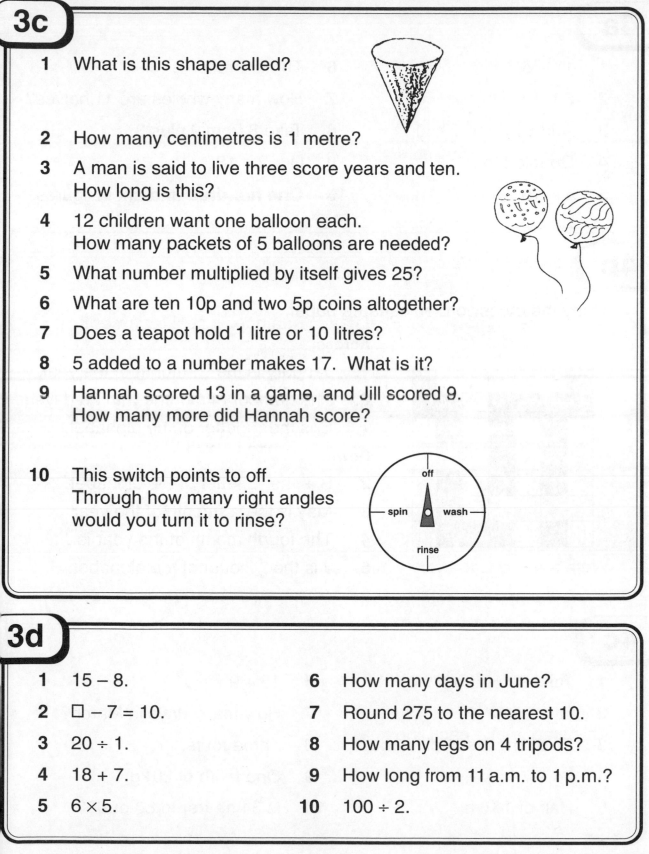

2   How many centimetres is 1 metre?

3   A man is said to live three score years and ten.
    How long is this?

4   12 children want one balloon each.
    How many packets of 5 balloons are needed?

5   What number multiplied by itself gives 25?

6   What are ten 10p and two 5p coins altogether?

7   Does a teapot hold 1 litre or 10 litres?

8   5 added to a number makes 17. What is it?

9   Hannah scored 13 in a game, and Jill scored 9.
    How many more did Hannah score?

10 This switch points to off.
    Through how many right angles
    would you turn it to rinse?

off

spin   wash

rinse

3d

1   15 − 8.

2   ☐ − 7 = 10.

3   20 ÷ 1.

4   18 + 7.

5   6 × 5.

6   How many days in June?

7   Round 275 to the nearest 10.

8   How many legs on 4 tripods?

9   How long from 11 a.m. to 1 p.m.?

10 100 ÷ 2.

4a

1. $17 - 8$.
2. $60 \div 2$.
3. Add £1.50 to £3.50.
4. Double ten.
5. $4 + 19$.
6. Three threes.
7. How many wholes are 11 halves?
8. Take 8 from 9 plus 3.
9. $\square \times 2 = 18$.
10. **One hundred and six** in figures.

4b

Copy the crossword on squared paper.

Across

1. January is the … month of the year.
6. The number of months with 28 days.
7. C is the … letter of the alphabet.

Down

2. B is the … letter of the alphabet.
3. May is the … month of the year.
4. The fourth month of the year is ….
5. J is the … letter of the alphabet.

4c

1. Take £2.50 from £4.
2. $\square \div 5 = 6$.
3. Five times four, plus one.
4. $14 - 7$.
5. Half of 16 cm.
6. $15 + 9$.
7. How many days in March?
8. Three fours.
9. One tenth of 20 kg.
10. Is 84 nearer to 80 or 90?

Treasure island

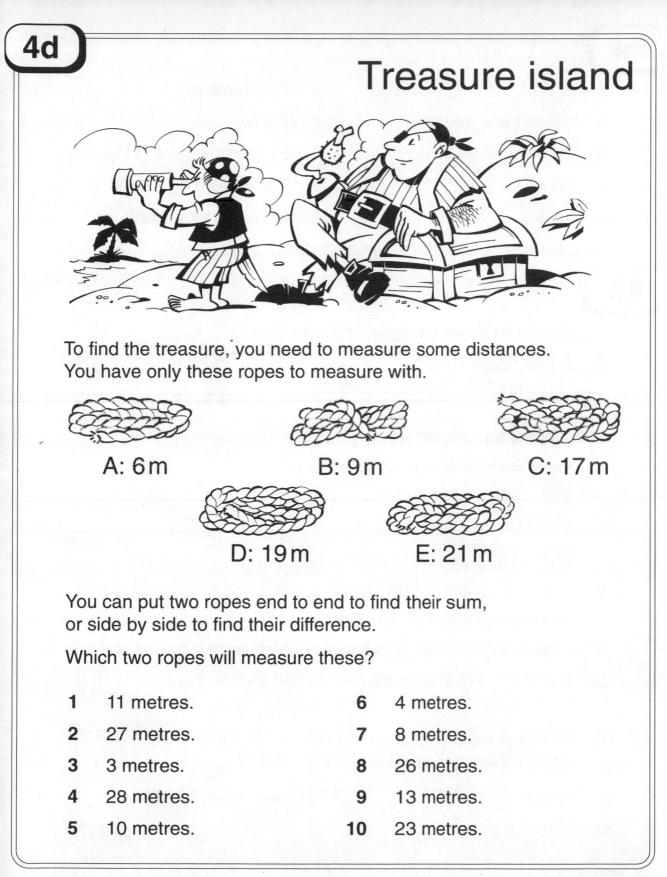

To find the treasure, you need to measure some distances.
You have only these ropes to measure with.

A: 6 m   B: 9 m   C: 17 m

D: 19 m   E: 21 m

You can put two ropes end to end to find their sum,
or side by side to find their difference.

Which two ropes will measure these?

1	11 metres.		**6**	4 metres.
2	27 metres.		**7**	8 metres.
3	3 metres.		**8**	26 metres.
4	28 metres.		**9**	13 metres.
5	10 metres.		**10**	23 metres.

5a

1	8 + 14.	**6**	One tenth of £1.
2	13 minus 8, minus 3.	**7**	7×5.
3	How many 2s in 16?	**8**	How many days in February?
4	$90 \div \square = 9$.	**9**	7 multiplied by 2, plus 3.
5	15 – 7.	**10**	One less than 1000.

5b

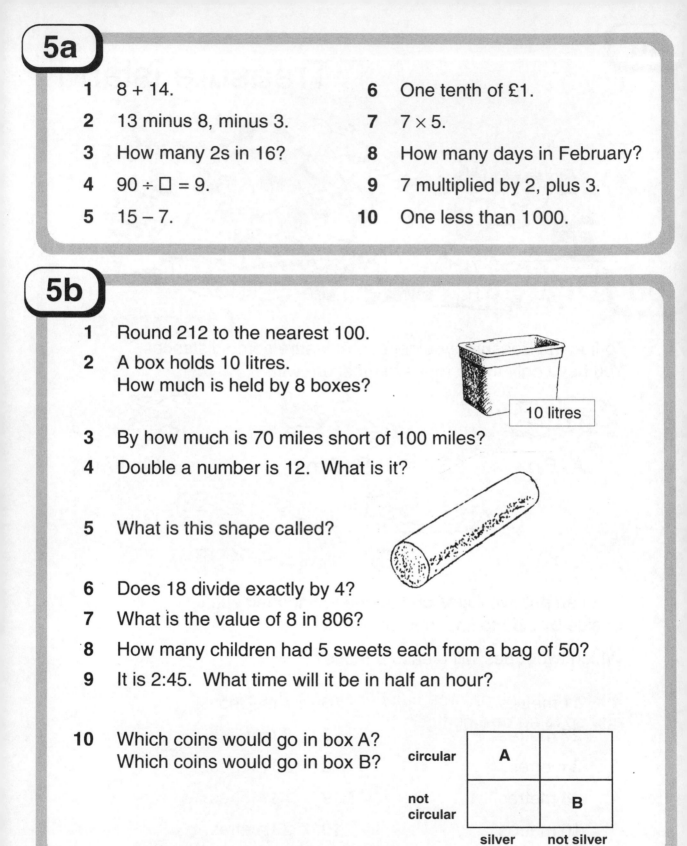

1 Round 212 to the nearest 100.

2 A box holds 10 litres.
How much is held by 8 boxes?

10 litres

3 By how much is 70 miles short of 100 miles?

4 Double a number is 12. What is it?

5 What is this shape called?

6 Does 18 divide exactly by 4?

7 What is the value of 8 in 806?

8 How many children had 5 sweets each from a bag of 50?

9 It is 2:45. What time will it be in half an hour?

10 Which coins would go in box A?
Which coins would go in box B?

	silver	not silver
circular	A	
not circular		B

5c

1 Add 4 and 4 and 4.	**6** One fifth of 15.
2 16 + 7.	**7** Subtract 10 from 46.
3 80 ÷ 2.	**8** Which is less: 106 or 160?
4 2 times 5 times 5.	**9** If ◆ × ◆ = 16, what is ◆?
5 18 – 9.	**10** One half of 24 km.

5d

Oddities

Copy the grid.

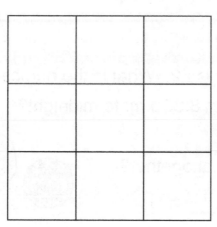

Use each of the numbers 1 to 9.
Write one number in every box.

Make each line of three numbers in any direction
add up to an **odd** number.

1 2 3 4 5 6 7 8 9

6a

1 Which two have a sum of twenty: 13, 6, 15, 7?

2 Round 478 to the nearest 100.

3 How many pairs can be made from 17 socks?

4 A jug holds 1.5 litres. What do 2 jugs hold?

5 What is the difference between a century and a score?

6 Jo has 3p more than Harry, who has 9p. How much has Jo?

7 What is the name of this shape?

8 Double a number is 22. What is the number?

9 How long is it from 8:30 p.m. to midnight?

10 How much is this altogether?

6b

1 14 − 9.

2 Half the sum of 4 and 10.

3 5 times 10, plus 3.

4 □ × 7 = 35.

5 9 + 17.

6 Eight fives.

7 38 + 10.

8 One more than 1009.

9 How many shoes are 11 pairs?

10 50 ÷ 2.

Magic squares

In a magic square, the three numbers in each row, column and diagonal add up to the same total.

Copy and complete these magic squares.

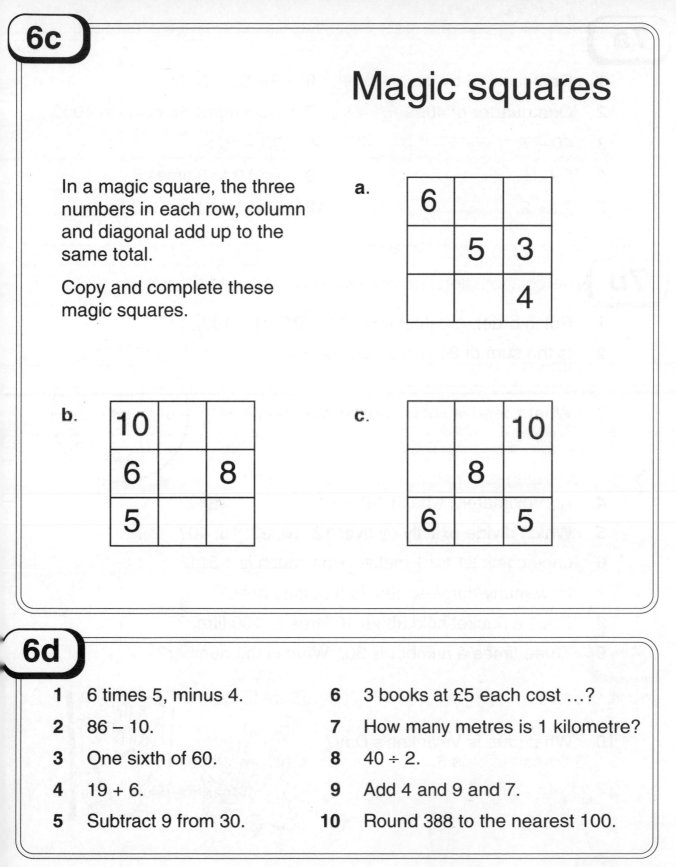

a.

6		
	5	3
		4

b.

10		
6		8
5		

c.

		10
	8	
6		5

6d

1	6 times 5, minus 4.	**6**	3 books at £5 each cost …?
2	86 – 10.	**7**	How many metres is 1 kilometre?
3	One sixth of 60.	**8**	40 ÷ 2.
4	19 + 6.	**9**	Add 4 and 9 and 7.
5	Subtract 9 from 30.	**10**	Round 388 to the nearest 100.

7a

1 Decrease 17 by 9.
2 One quarter of 40.
3 40 − 7.
4 5 + 16.
5 22 ÷ 2.

6 9 × 5.
7 How many 5p coins in 40p?
8 93 + 10.
9 Add 2 to 8 times 5.
10 One less than 1030.

7b

1 Put in order, greatest first: 110, 101, 111, 100.

2 Is the sum of 30 and 50 odd or even?

3 What speed is shown on this speedometer?

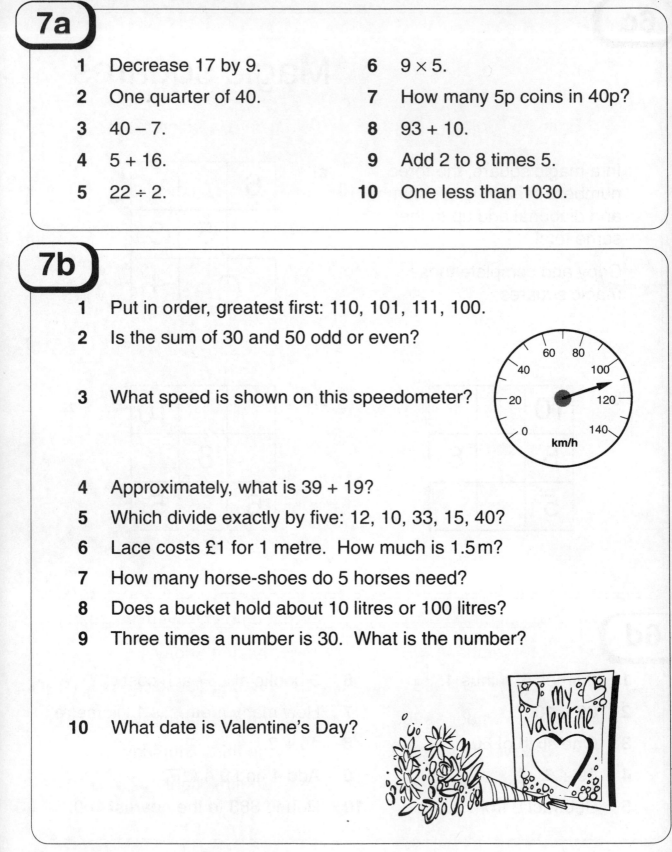

4 Approximately, what is 39 + 19?

5 Which divide exactly by five: 12, 10, 33, 15, 40?

6 Lace costs £1 for 1 metre. How much is 1.5m?

7 How many horse-shoes do 5 horses need?

8 Does a bucket hold about 10 litres or 100 litres?

9 Three times a number is 30. What is the number?

10 What date is Valentine's Day?

7c

1	14 – 8.	**6**	50 – 9.
2	One fifth of 50.	**7**	Which is greater: 789 or 798?
3	From 76 subtract 10.	**8**	What date is Boxing Day?
4	200 ÷ 2	**9**	18 + 8.
5	5 multiplied by 6.	**10**	Take 7 from 5 times 4.

7d

Calendars

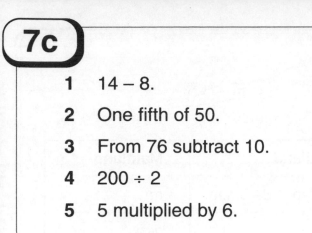

Friday
November
13th
1998

1 What day of the week is:

   a. 20 November 1998

   b. 7 November 1998

   c. 29 November 1998

   d. 13 November 1999

   e. 13 November 2000

2 What date in November 1998 is:

   a. the first Friday

   b. the first Tuesday

   c. the last Saturday

   d. the third Thursday

   e. Bonfire Night

8a

A ferry goes from the island to the mainland and back again three times a day. It takes 45 minutes each way.

The ferry always waits at the jetty for half an hour so that people can get on and off.

Island	Mainland
dep. 8:15 a.m.	arr.
arr.	dep.
dep.	arr.
arr.	dep.
dep.	arr.
arr.	dep.

The first ferry goes at 8:15 a.m.

Copy and complete the timetable for the ferry.

8b

Draw two squares.

Use each of the numbers 1 to 6 once.
Write them in the squares.

The sum of the numbers in one square must be twice the sum of the numbers in the other square.

Do it in four different ways.

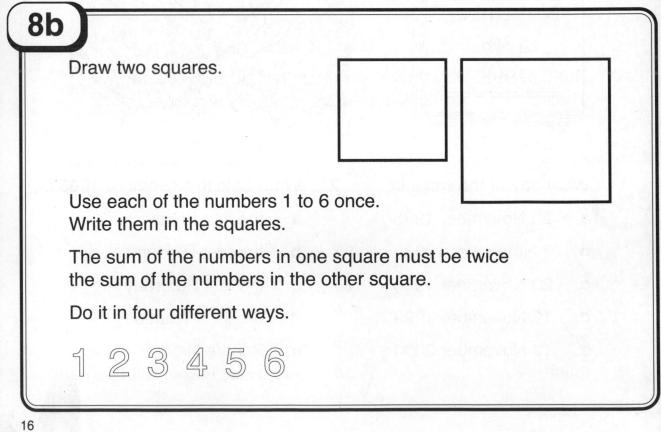

1 2 3 4 5 6

8c

1 1 m of string is cut into quarters. How long is each piece?

2 Face east, then turn through 180°.
Which direction do you face now?

3 What fraction is ringed?

4 A ball costs 15p. What change do you get from 50p?

5 Which area is larger: a postage stamp or a thumb-print?

6 If 5 cm is cut from 1 m of ribbon, what length is left?

7 The final score in a netball match was 15–9.
What was the difference in the scores?

8 What time was it 30 minutes ago?

9 Is the height of a lamp-post about 10 m or 100 m?

10 Ruth, Ajit and Sam share 20 sweets as fairly as they can.
They give the rest to Karen. How many does she get?

8d

1	16 – 9.		6	Round 67 to the nearest 100.
2	Is 201 odd or even?		7	Find the sum of 5, 9 and 4.
3	5 + 19.		8	84 + 20.
4	24 ÷ 2.		9	Increase 37 by 3.
5	5 times 7.		10	How many grams is 1 kilogram?

Crack the code

Foreign spies write messages in code.
They use numbers to stand for letters.

1 is A, 2 is B, and so on.
You will need to work out the rest.

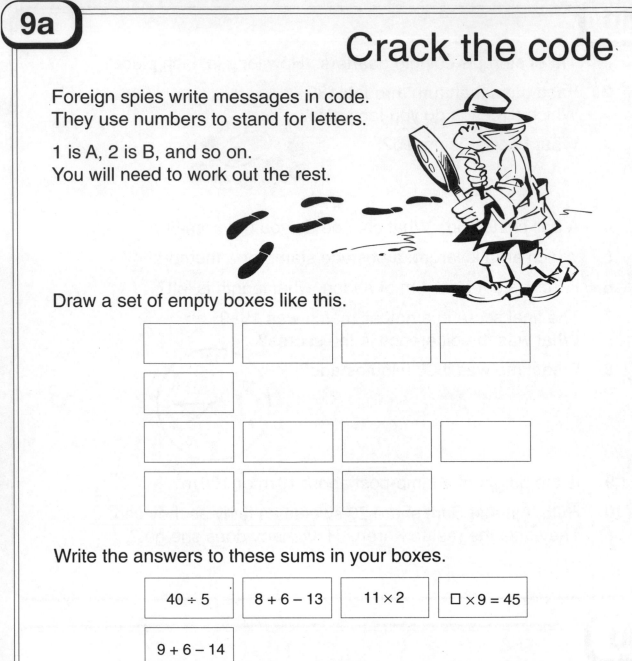

Draw a set of empty boxes like this.

Write the answers to these sums in your boxes.

$40 \div 5$	$8 + 6 - 13$	11×2	$\square \times 9 = 45$
$9 + 6 - 14$			
$20 - 6$	$17 - \square = 8$	$16 - 9 - 4$	$\blacklozenge \times \blacklozenge = 25$
$12 \div 3$	$10 \div 10$	$8 + 7 + 10$	

Now work out the spy's message!

9b

Copy and complete these to make each sum correct.
Each time write two + and two − signs instead of the boxes.

a. $5 \boxplus 3 \boxminus 1 \boxplus 3 \boxminus 5 = 5$ ✔

b. $12 \boxminus 3 \boxplus 4 \boxminus 5 \boxplus 6 = 14$ ✔

9   13   8   14

9c

1   How many rectangles altogether?
2   What is next: 35, 25, 15, 5 …?
3   How many 5p coins make £1?
4   Which is greatest: 637, 736, 673 or 763?
5   How much later is midnight than 6:00 p.m.?
6   How many millilitres is half a litre?
7   Add 3 to the difference between 5 and 9.
8   Tickets are £5 each. How many can you get for £28?
9   The side of a square is 2 cm. How far is it all round the edge?
10   What is the total of three 2p and four 5p coins?

9d

1   19 + 8.
2   One tenth of 60.
3   42 ÷ 2.
4   Add three to seven fives.
5   14 − 6.

6   From the sum of 2 and 22, take 4.
7   Two less than 179.
8   5 × 8.
9   87 − 20.
10   Round 352 to the nearest 10.

10a

1	67 – 3.	**6**	15 – 9.
2	Add 8 to half of 8.	**7**	What is next: 15, 11, 7, 3 …?
3	6 + 17.	**8**	Which is more: 309 or 390?
4	Decrease 50 by 6.	**9**	66 ÷ 2.
5	391 + 100.	**10**	Which four coins make 76p?

10b

1 My 3 hens have 10 chicks each. How many chicks do I have?

2 What is left over when 52 is divided by 10?

3 Through how many degrees would
you turn this switch from high to low?

4 What is half way between 11 and 19?

5 Which two differ by twenty: 76, 46, 56, 86?

6 Roughly how long is your lunch break?

7 What fraction of these spots are ringed?

8 What shape is a side face of a pyramid?

9 What are eleven 10p coins altogether?

10 What temperature is it?

10c

1 Add 5 and 5 and 5.
2 16 − 8.
3 Decrease 167 by 10.
4 30 ÷ 5.
5 18 + 5.

6 Add two threes to eighteen.
7 275 plus 200.
8 Which three coins make 90p?
9 What is next: 13, 18, 23, 28 …?
10 One more than 999.

10d

In this 2 × 2 square the numbers add up to 10.

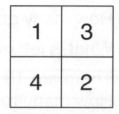

Copy and complete these two grids.

a. Make each 2 × 2 square add up to 15.

			6
			1
			3
1	7	0	4

b. Make each 2 × 2 square add up to 20.

6	4	7	1
5			
2			
3			

11a

1. How many children can have 5 sweets each from a bag of 27?

2. If you spend half of 50p, what is left?

3. What shape is the base of a cylinder?

4. There are 13 scones on a plate. If the cat steals one, how many each can the twins have?

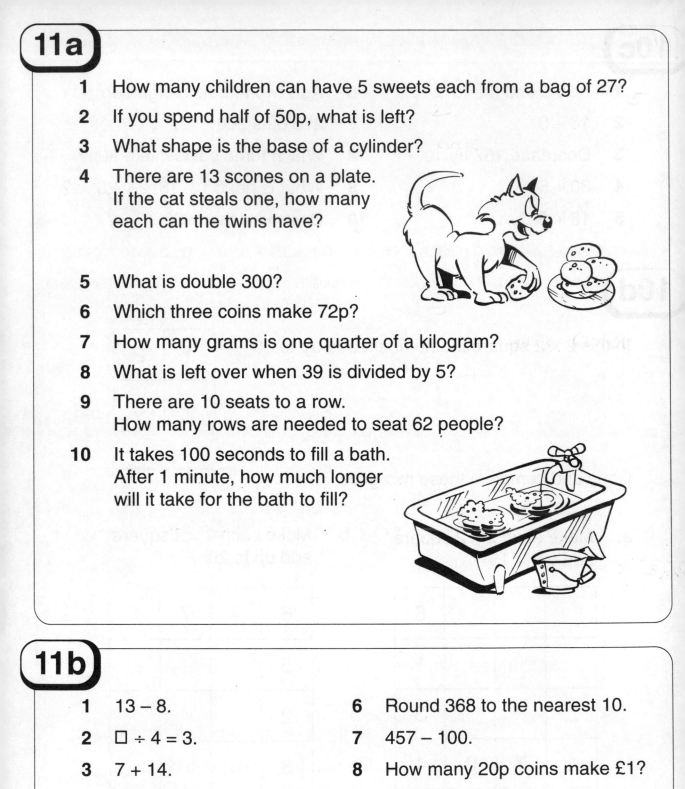

5. What is double 300?

6. Which three coins make 72p?

7. How many grams is one quarter of a kilogram?

8. What is left over when 39 is divided by 5?

9. There are 10 seats to a row. How many rows are needed to seat 62 people?

10. It takes 100 seconds to fill a bath. After 1 minute, how much longer will it take for the bath to fill?

11b

1. $13 - 8$.

2. $\square \div 4 = 3$.

3. $7 + 14$.

4. Half of 62.

5. 5×9.

6. Round 368 to the nearest 10.

7. $457 - 100$.

8. How many 20p coins make £1?

9. $35 \div 5$.

10. Take 2 times 6 from 15.

11c

1	16 + 6.	**6**	Subtract 45 minutes from 1 hour.
2	5×0.	**7**	One quarter of 84.
3	Increase 37 by 10.	**8**	What shape is a can of coke?
4	446 – 200.	**9**	40 – 5.
5	97 minus 5.	**10**	Which is less: £1.09 or £1.90?

11d

| 2 | 2 | | 2 | 5 | | 5 | 4 |

In this set of three dominoes: the first is a double;

touching sides match;

all three dominoes are different;

the numbers add up to 20.

Draw three blank dominoes. Write numbers from 1 to 6 on them.

In your set of three dominoes: the first must be a double;

touching sides must match;

all three dominoes must be different;

the numbers must add up to 20.

Find eight different ways of doing it altogether.

12a

1. How many degrees is one right angle?

2. Does a pear weigh about 150 g or 1.5 kg?

3. If 1 kg of apples costs 80p, what do 2 kg cost?

4. What is left over when 49 is divided by 5?

5. Which is smallest: 345, 433 or 354?

6. What is the number nearest to 39 that divides exactly by 4?

7. If you spend three quarters of 40p, what change do you get?

8. What number less than 30 divides exactly by both 3 and 5?

9. Find the difference between 8 and 26.

10. What fraction of this shape is shaded?

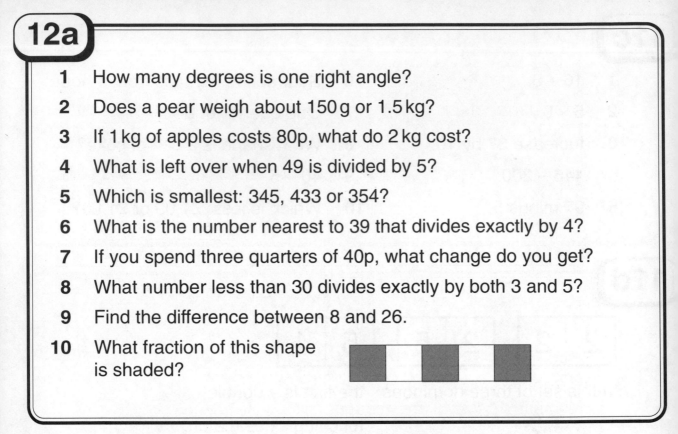

12b

Copy this grid.

Cross out just two numbers.

1	2	4	8
5	3	2	3
7	7	1	6
2	6	3	9

The sum of the rest of the numbers
in each row and column must divide exactly by 5.

12c

1 11×5.
2 One quarter of 24.
3 $8 + 17$.
4 Three quarters of 80.
5 $237 - 10$.
6 Half of 22.
7 Round 405 to the nearest 10.
8 What shape is a beach ball?
9 Write 267p in pounds and pence.
10 $45 \div 5$.

12d

1 What shape is the base of a cone?
2 What are four £1 and three 10p coins altogether?
3 There are 4 chews in a packet.
   How many packets are needed
   to give 21 children one chew each?
4 How many 5s added together make 35?
5 Tara worked out the cost of 4 books at 90p each .
   Her calculator showed 360. What was the answer?
6 Which is colder: $-3\,°C$ or $-5\,°C$?
7 How much are 20 books at £3 each?
8 Write **two thousand, one hundred and one** in figures.
9 Ben grilled 12 fish fingers. How many people had 3 each?
10 How many triangles
   can you see altogether?

On the bus

This graph shows how many people went on a 40-seater bus from 8:00 a.m. to 5:00 p.m.

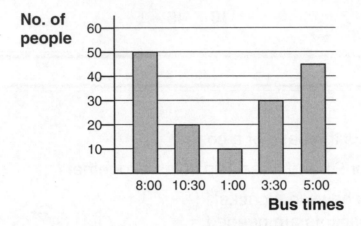

1   The journey to town takes 20 minutes.
    Which bus should you get to be there by 11 a.m.?

2   If you miss the 3:30 bus, how much later is the next one?

3   How many people went on the last bus of the day?

4   Did more people go on the bus before or after midday?

5   How many people had to stand on the 8:00 bus?

6   How many had to stand on the 5:00 bus?

7   How many empty seats were there on the 1:00 bus?

8   The bus fare is 50p.
    What was the cost of all the tickets on the 1:00 bus?

9   How many people caught the bus between 10:00 and 4:00?

10 How many bus seats are there altogether each day?

13b

The milkman left 18 bottles of milk in Lime Street.

Each house had some milk.

Some houses had 5 bottles.

The rest had 2 bottles each.

How many houses are there in Lime Street?

13c

1 Four story tapes cost £12. How much is one?
2 How many seconds in three quarters of a minute?
3 How much milk is there in 10 half-litre bottles?
4 Round 397 to the nearest 10.
5 Divide 30 by 5, then divide that by 3.
6 How many 50 cm ribbons can be cut from 3 m?
7 How many faces has a square-based pyramid?
8 Approximately, what is the sum of 29 and 49?
9 What is left over when 5 children share 37p equally?
10 Which three coins make 57p?

13d

1 $90 \div 3$.
2 Add 6 and 6 and 6.
3 Ten minus four plus six.
4 $8 + \square + 4 = 15$.
5 Find the product of 5 and 6.
6 Is 148 nearer to 100 or 200?
7 Subtract 8 from 70.
8 Add 3×3 to 3×2.
9 $21 - 5$.
10 Take 3×4 from 20.

14a

1. $19 + 9$.
2. Two fifths of 50.
3. Add 20 to 450.
4. $\square + 7 - 3 = 16$.
5. $31 + 32$.
6. If $20 \blacklozenge 2 = 40$, what is $\blacklozenge$?
7. Take 15 seconds from 1 minute.
8. Write **one half** as a decimal.
9. How many 20p coins make £5?
10. Write 850 to the nearest 100.

14b

1. What is the cost of 9 bags of potatoes at 50p a bag?
2. Which is fewer: 120, 110 or 201 sweets?
3. What colour is the 27th bead in this pattern?

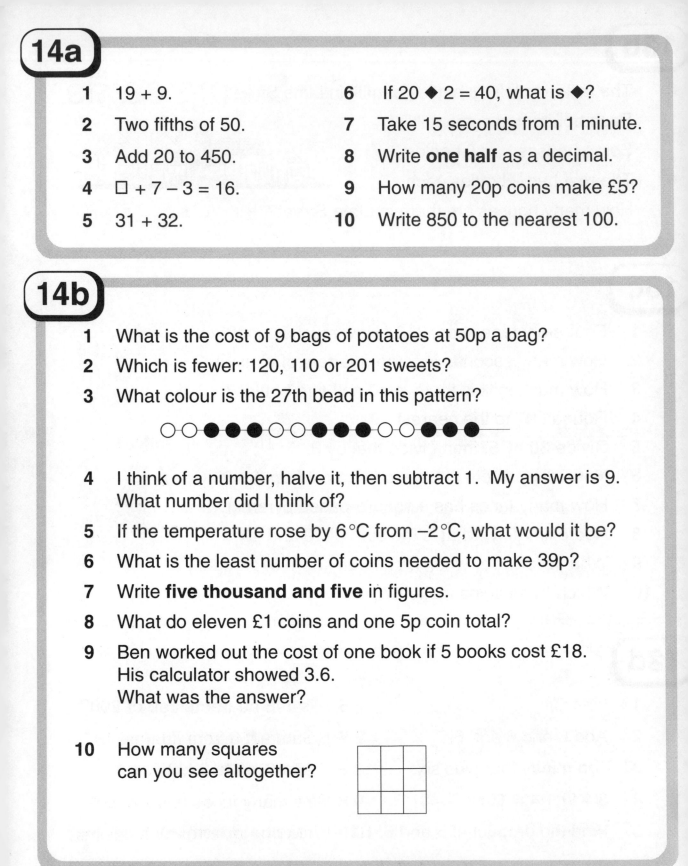

4. I think of a number, halve it, then subtract 1. My answer is 9. What number did I think of?
5. If the temperature rose by 6°C from −2°C, what would it be?
6. What is the least number of coins needed to make 39p?
7. Write **five thousand and five** in figures.
8. What do eleven £1 coins and one 5p coin total?
9. Ben worked out the cost of one book if 5 books cost £18. His calculator showed 3.6. What was the answer?
10. How many squares can you see altogether?

14c

Stamp cards

Draw a blank 4 × 4 grid.

This is your stamp card.

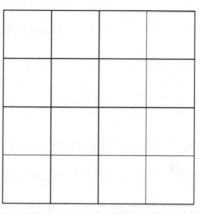

Imagine you have four 1p, four 2p, four 3p and four 4p stamps.

One stamp must be stuck in each space on the card.

The total of each row, column and diagonal must be 10p.

Write the values of the stamps in the spaces.

14d

1   9 + 18.

2   Two fifths of 25.

3   35 – 20.

4   How many cm in 1.45 m?

5   236 + 10.

6   What three coins make £1.01?

7   Round 975 to the nearest 10.

8   If 16 ◆ 5 = 21, what is ◆?

9   How many faces has a cube?

10   Write **one quarter** as a decimal.

15a

1	22 + 8.	**6**	What shape is a house brick?
2	32 − 30.	**7**	Approximately, what is 29 + 52?
3	5 + 17.	**8**	Which four coins make 77p?
4	Write 226 cm in metres.	**9**	Write **nine tenths** as a decimal.
5	348 − 10.	**10**	Write 151 to the nearest 100.

15b

1 What whole numbers are less than 502 but more than 498?

2 How many cakes at 50p each can be bought for £4.50?

3 What position in this line would the 6th white bead be?

4 How many hours from 4 p.m. to midnight?

5 What number is half way between 16 and 26?

6 It cost Yasmin £1.30 to post two letters.
One cost 30p more than the other.
What did each letter cost?

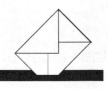

7 What are six £1 and two 2p coins altogether?

8 Roughly, how heavy are 7 sacks of corn if each weighs 19 kg?

9 Choc-drops are 3 for 5p. How many do you get for 15p?

10 Mum had 22 apples and some empty baskets.
She put 7 apples in some baskets and 2 in each of the others.
How many baskets were there?

15c

1. Is 300 odd or even?
2. $100 - 75$.
3. How many cm in 1.4 m?
4. $19 + 19$.
5. One less than 3170.
6. How many edges has a cube?
7. What is next: 2, 4, 8, 16 …?
8. Approximately, what is $21 + 48$?
9. Can you make £1 with 3 coins?
10. $\square \times 11 = 110$.

15d

Magic triangles

The three numbers along each side of a magic triangle add up to the same magic number.

Copy the diagram.

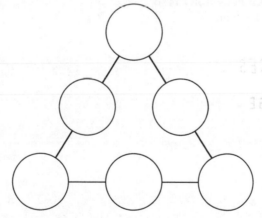

Use each of the numbers 1, 2, 3, 5, 6 and 7.
Write them in the circles to make 10 the magic number.

Now do it to make 14 the magic number .

1 2 3 and 5 6 7

Published by the Press Syndicate of the University of Cambridge
The Pitt Building, Trumpington Street, Cambridge CB2 1RP
40 West 20th Street, New York, NY 10011–4211, USA
10 Stamford Road, Oakleigh, Melbourne 3166, Australia

First published 1994
Third printing 1996

Printed in Great Britain by Scotprint Ltd, Musselburgh

A catalogue record for this book is available from the British Library.

ISBN 0 521 48552 5   paperback

Cover illustration by Tony Hall
Cartoons by Tim Sell

Notice to teachers
It is illegal to reproduce any part of this work in material form
(including photocopying and electronic storage) except under the
following circumstances:
(i)   where you are abiding by a licence granted to your school by
      the Copyright Licensing Agency;
(ii) where no such licence exists, or where you wish to exceed the
      terms of a licence, and you have gained the written permission
      of Cambridge University Press;
(iii) where you are allowed to reproduce without permission under
      the provisions of Chapter 3 of the Copyright, Designs and
      Patents Act 1988.